WORKING STEAM

Collett Castles & Kings

Roy Hobbs

Ian Allan
PUBLISHING

Introduction

At the beginning of the last century GWR Chief Mechanical Engineer G. J. Churchward had carried out investigations into compounding, importing a 4-4-2 four-cylinder locomotive of this type from France to compare its performance with that of the pair of simple two-cylinder 4-6-0s he had introduced into service at around the same time, in 1903. He found that there was little significant difference in performance between the two types, although smoother running and reduced wear on the track was experienced with the compound, due to the improved balance of the reciprocating parts provided by four cylinders.

Following trials with a four-cylinder simple, No 40 (later named *North Star*), built in 1906 as a 4-4-2 but later converted to a 4-6-0 (as No 4000) to improve adhesion, the outcome was the introduction between 1907 and 1923 of a further 72 'Star' 4-6-0s, Nos 4001-72. During this period Churchward retired, being replaced as CME by C. B. Collett, who took over the reins in 1922.

Churchward had earlier suggested an increase in boiler size on the 'Stars', together with the 'Saint' two-cylinder 4-6-0s, but this had been vetoed by the Civil Engineer on weight grounds. Collett, therefore, set about producing a compromise boiler design; his new 'Castle' type was based on the 'Star' but featured a rear frame extension, allowing a more commodious cab and a slightly increased boiler diameter, with similarly enlarged cylinders and an extended firebox.

The initial batch of 10 engines, Nos 4073-82, was constructed in 1923/4. In subsequent years 15 'Stars' were rebuilt as 'Castles', commencing with No 4009 *Shooting Star* (later No 100A1 *Lloyd's*) in April 1925 and concluding with Nos 4063-72 (renumbered to Nos 5083-92) between 1937 and 1940; the solitary 4-6-2, No 111 *The Great Bear*, had been dealt with earlier, in 1924, being renamed *Viscount Churchill* on conversion. The main number series finally comprised Nos 4073-99, 5000-99 and 7000-37, and with rebuilds the class totalled some 171 examples. The last 40 locomotives were constructed postwar under the jurisdiction of F. W. Hawksworth, who had succeeded Collett as CME in 1941.

Following bridge upgrading on the London–Plymouth route in 1926 to take a 22½-ton axle load, Collett was able to put in hand the design of an even more powerful express locomotive. This resulted in the 'King' class, and the first of these, No 6000 *King George V*, appeared in June 1927; a further increase in boiler diameter together with raised pressure from 225lb to 250lb, plus a reduction in coupled wheel diameter to 6ft 6in, enabled nominal tractive effort to reach 40,300lb, making it then the most powerful locomotive in the country.

The prototype was completed in record time, enabling it to appear at the Baltimore & Ohio Railroad centenary celebrations in September 1927, when it was presented with the bell it still carries today. A total of 30 'Kings', Nos 6000-29, were constructed between

Front cover: Heading a Paddington–Plymouth excursion on Sunday 11 September 1960, No 6029 *King Edward VIII* is held by signals at Tigley as it waits to cross over to the up line during single-line working resulting from weekend maintenance. *Peter W. Gray*

Back cover: The classic view at Teignmouth station as 'Castle' No 5059 *Earl of Aldwyn* departs with the northbound 'Devonian', the 9.15am Paignton–Bradford (Forster Square), on 2 July 1957. *R. C. Riley*

Previous page: Seen near Hungerford, 'Castle' No 5075 *Wellington*, so named in 1940 after the famous World War 2 bomber, is depicted with the up 'Torbay Express' on 4 July 1959; the locomotive's original name, *Devizes Castle*, was reused on newly constructed No 7002 in June 1946. A Wolverhampton Division engine for much of the postwar era, No 5075 enjoyed spells at Exeter (83C) and Neath (87A) in the early 1960s, eventually being withdrawn from Bristol Bath Road (82A) in September 1962. *R. C. Riley*

First published 2006

ISBN (10) 0 7110 3132 0
ISBN (13) 978 0 7110 3132 6

© Ian Allan Publishing Ltd 2006

Published by Ian Allan Publishing

an imprint of Ian Allan Publishing Ltd, Hersham, Surrey, KT12 4RG
Printed in England by Ian Allan Printing Ltd, Hersham, Surrey, KT12 4RG

Code: 0610/A2

Visit the Ian Allan Publishing website at www.ianallanpublishing.com

1927 and 1930, all named after British monarchs; originally these ranged, in reverse order, from *King George V* to *King Stephen*, but the last two were subsequently renamed to recognise later accessions.

During the Hawksworth regime various trials were undertaken with superheaters, and in February 1948 a four-row version was installed on No 6022 *King Edward III*. This produced evidence of much improved steaming, and between 1951 and 1955 the entire class was converted. Additionally, following revised draughting arrangements introduced in the autumn of 1952, further experiments were carried out in September 1955 with No 6015 *King Richard III*, by introducing a twin-orifice blastpipe and double chimney. These changes produced such a marked gain in overall performance that, on one trial run to Plymouth, the locomotive reputedly achieved a maximum of 108.5mph near Patney, an average of 107.5mph being sustained over three-quarters of a mile. Although the precise figures have been disputed, they nevertheless represent the highest maxima recorded by any GWR locomotive. Conversion of the remainder of the class followed in the years 1955-8.

A comparable programme with the 'Castles' commenced in May 1956, when No 7018 *Dryslwyn Castle* was fitted with a double chimney in conjunction with its existing three-row superheater, and resulted in a similar improvement in performance. Following this success No 4090 *Dorchester Castle* was converted in 1957, but here the combination included a four-row superheater, the outcome being an extremely free-running engine. This led to the conversion of a further 64 'Castles', No 7018 being further rebuilt to this standard in April 1958.

With the progressive march of 'dieselisation' from the late 1950s the main duties of both classes gradually disappeared, and in December 1962 the surviving four members of the 'King' class were officially withdrawn, although No 6018 was retained until April 1963 to work a commemorative special from Birmingham to Swindon. In June 1965 three of the four remaining active 'Castles' were retired, leaving only No 7029 *Clun Castle*, scheduled for private preservation, in service at the close of WR steam operation in the following December.

However, this was not destined to be the finale, as, on withdrawal, pioneer No 4073 *Caerphilly Castle* was presented for display at the Science Museum; it was eventually transferred to STEAM: Museum of the Great Western Railway, where it can now be seen along with No 6000 *King George V*. Besides these a further two 'Kings' and five 'Castles' have been rescued from the well-known Barry scrapyard, and, of these, four have since been returned to operational condition.

In compiling this album a variety of reference sources have been used where my own knowledge was incomplete, and amongst these I would mention in particular *Great Loco Story* by R. L. Grey (Quadrant Publications, 1947), *The GWR Stars, Castles and Kings* by O. S. Nock (David & Charles, 1967/70), *Great Western 4-6-0s at Work* by Michael Rutherford (Ian Allan Publishing, 1995) and various RCTS publications, along with monthlies *The Railway Magazine*, *Trains Illustrated*, *Steam Days*, *Steam World* and the RCTS *Railway Observer*. Several photographers have been kind enough to assist with assembling a representative selection of views of these engines in service, and all are individually credited as appropriate. The contribution of the late R. C. (Dick) Riley and Trevor Owen, who between them provided the greater part of the material used are especially noted without their substantial help this volume would have been much the poorer. My thanks also to David Clark, for use of photographs from the collection of the late Kenneth Wightman. It is, however, to Dick that this album is dedicated. An invaluable help with my earlier projects, he was a friend for many years, and his recent death is sorely felt. He leaves a gap that will be hard to fill, but fortunately we still have his many books, articles and photographs by which to remember a life devoted to increasing our knowledge of railways.

Roy Hobbs
Exeter
September 2006

Right: The immediate forerunner of the 'Castle' class, and the design upon which the Collett type was based, was Churchward's 'Star' 4-6-0, represented here by No 4056 *Princess Margaret* at Old Oak Common on 23 September 1956. Constructed in 1914, this locomotive was the last member of its class to remain in service, finally being withdrawn from Landore (87E) depot in October 1957. The more basic style of cab and the elbow-pattern steam pipes will be noted. *R. C. Riley*

The first of the 'Castle' class, No 4073 *Caerphilly Castle*, at Old Oak Common on 2 June 1961, following restoration to near-original condition for exhibition at the Science Museum. It is shown awaiting road transfer to the latter's premises at South Kensington, the buffers having been covered with sacking to prevent damage in transit. Whilst the original type of 3,500gal tender has been reinstated, changes to the locomotive's appearance as built include later-pattern inside-cylinder piston-valve covers, a shorter chimney and the omission of the original bogie brakes. Constructed in August 1923, it was withdrawn in May 1960, having completed just over 1.91 million miles in service; it ended its career at Cardiff Canton (86C), having spent the early 1950s at Bristol Bath Road (82A). Following several years on display at the Science Museum it would move to Didcot Railway Centre, later being transferred to STEAM: Museum of the Great Western Railway. *R. C. Riley*

Having left Paddington with the 1.45pm to Worcester, No 4088 *Dartmouth Castle* approaches Royal Oak on 30 August 1958. Built in July 1925, it would remain in service until May 1964. A double chimney had been installed, together with four-row superheater, during a works visit some three months earlier, in May 1958. Among exceptional runs recorded was one on the 6.10pm Paddington–Birmingham service during Whitsun 1930, when, with a load of 440 tons tare (475 tons gross), a speed of 52.5mph was recorded at Ardley Summit, with a maximum of 83.5mph at Haddenham, whilst Hatton Bank was breasted at 32mph. Following nationalisation it was based on the Newton Abbot Division until the late 1950s, subsequently being allocated to Worcester (85A) depot and, finally Bristol St Philips Marsh (82B) prior to withdrawal. *R. C. Riley*

With the red lion identifying the Harrow Road hostelry just visible above Westbourne Bridge, No 7011 *Banbury Castle* departs Paddington with the 'Cathedrals Express', the 2.45pm to Worcester and Hereford, on 9 September 1961. After initial allocation to Bristol Bath Road (82A) depot, following completion in June 1948, No 7011 had moved to Shrewsbury (84G) by 1959, after which it saw service at a variety of depots including Cardiff Canton (88A), Worcester (85A) and Reading (81D), before returning to Worcester and finally Oxley (then LMR 2B), from where it would be withdrawn in February 1965. It retained the single chimney throughout its working life. *R. C. Riley*

Right: The depot at Ranelagh Bridge, a short distance from Paddington station, enabled the convenient turning and servicing of locomotives before they took up their return working. No 6023 *King Edward II* awaits its next duty, the 3.55pm to Pembroke Dock, on 10 September 1960. Following June 1962 withdrawal it would be sent to the legendary Barry scrapyard that December. Despite the drastic severing of one pair of driving wheels after shunting incident there it was rescued in December 1984 and is currently under restoration at the Didcot base of the Great Western Society. *R. C. Riley*

Right: No 4086 *Builth Castle* over the ash pit at Old Oak Common (81A) depot on 25 September 1955. During July 1939 this locomotive achieved a measure of fame when it was timed at 100mph down the 1-in-100 bank past Honeybourne on the 12.45pm Worcester service, described as 'the first properly authenticated record of this speed on a GWR train in normal everyday service', according to Cecil J. Allen, writing in the February 1940 issue of *The Railway Magazine*. Although shown here based at Plymouth Laira (83D), it moved around various depots in the BR era, serving Worcester, Newton Abbot, Bristol, Cardiff and London divisions in turn, being withdrawn from Reading (81D) in April 1962. *Trevor Owen*

Left: No 4080 *Powderham Castle* in charge of the down 'Capitals United Express' near Old Oak Common on 13 August 1960. The title was first applied in February 1956 to the 3.55pm to Swansea and 6.30am up working. However, for three days a week the down journey was extended to Fishguard Harbour to make a connection with the Cork steamer service, although no equivalent working was provided in the up direction. No 4080 was constructed in March 1924, being fitted with its double chimney, along with a four-row superheater, in August 1958. It worked primarily in the Bristol Division in the immediate postwar era but was later allocated to Newton Abbot (83A) and in the 1960s to Cardiff Canton (88A), before retirement from the London Division at Southall (81C) in August 1964. *R. C. Riley*

Below: Hanwell & Elthorne station is the location for a further named train, the 'Cheltenham Spa Express', headed by a resplendent No 7033 *Hartlebury Castle* on 6 October 1958. Illustrated here with a single chimney, the locomotive was to receive a double chimney in July 1959 but would nevertheless become the first of the Hawksworth '5098' series to be withdrawn in January 1963, having been based at Old Oak Common since completion in July 1950. The 2.40pm Cheltenham Spa–Paddington working became popularly known as the 'Cheltenham Flyer'; although shown in timetables as a 'Cheltenham Spa Express' this title never appeared on the locomotive or carriages and was shared by other similar daily services. The true 'Cheltenham Flyer' of the prewar era had been officially the world's fastest train, in 1932 covering the 77.3 miles from Swindon to Paddington in 65 minutes. The 'Cheltenham Spa Express' title was introduced in September 1956, when the 8.0am service was still covering the 91 miles between Kemble and Paddington in even time. *K. W. Wightman*

The 'Cathedrals Express' title was originally applied in September 1957 to the 7.45am Hereford–Paddington service and 4.45pm return, changing in November 1959 to the 9.50am Hereford departure and earlier 2.45pm working from London; the latter was booked non-stop to Oxford, covering the 63½ miles in 71 minutes. Here No 5037 *Monmouth Castle* passes the small airfield at White Waltham, visible in the background, with the down train on 8 August 1959; the Hawksworth-pattern tender will be noted. Constructed in May 1935, the locomotive was allocated postwar to various depots, including Old Oak Common (then PDN), Bristol Bath Road (82A), Worcester (85A) and later those in the Neath Division, finally being withdrawn from Bristol St Philips Marsh (82B) in March 1964. *Trevor Owen*

Among the final duties for some of the six 'King' 4-6-0s then remaining in service were the Newbury race specials of 27 October 1962. This view features either No 6005 *King George II* or No 6011 *King James I* near White Waltham with one of the three 'King'-hauled specials run that day, which also involved No 6000 *King George V*. On the previous day No 6000, along with No 6018 *King Henry VI*, had been chosen to head two VIP specials to Llanwern Steelworks, near Newport, for the official Royal opening, though the Royal Train itself was diesel-hauled for this event. The final four class members would all be withdrawn in December 1962, although No 6018 was to receive a stay of execution enabling it to undertake a celebratory journey, heading a final trip for the Stephenson Locomotive Society from Birmingham to Swindon via Greenford, in April 1963. *Roy Hobbs*

Left: No 7017 *G. J. Churchward* near Twyford with an up Class C parcels working on 10 September 1960. Built in August 1948 and officially named at Paddington on 29 October that year by the President of the Institution of Mechanical Engineers, this locomotive would be one of 13 Hawksworth 'Castles' to retain a single chimney until withdrawal in February 1963. On a notable run in the spring of 1960 with the 4.10pm Paddington–Birmingham — usually a 'King' duty — with an exceptional load of 14 coaches (grossing 520 tons) it arrived at Bicester only two minutes down, having earlier recorded a maximum of 80mph at Haddenham and sustained 64mph on the 1-in-200 climb to Brill Tunnel; further excellent work, with 'Hall' assistance up Hatton Bank, resulted in a 2min-early arrival in Birmingham. *K. W. Wightman*

Inset: Nameplate of No 7017. *John Wiltshire*

Below: An evening study west of Twyford on 29 July 1961, featuring No 5050 *Earl of St. Germans* with a down express bound for Fishguard. Until August 1937 this locomotive had been known as *Devizes Castle*, a name later allocated to No 7002, completed in June 1946. On all three days of the Cheltenham National Hunt race meeting in March 1954 No 5050 was noted at Swindon coupled to No 5040 *Stokesay Castle*, the pair heading the race excursion train from Paddington to Cheltenham. On 25 June 1963 it was observed taking a schools excursion from Bristol to Portsmouth but was then impounded at Fratton depot due to its use on an apparently unauthorised route; how it returned to Bristol is unrecorded. In the BR era it was based throughout the 1950s at Shrewsbury (84G) but after an interval at Old Oak Common (81A) was transferred to Bristol St Philips Marsh (82B) in 1961, from where it was withdrawn in August 1963. *Trevor Owen*

Above: Heading for Sonning Cutting from the Twyford direction, No 7020 *Gloucester Castle* has charge of a down express, comprising a rake of coaches in the carmine and cream livery used for main-line stock until this was succeeded, from around 1956, by the lined maroon livery seen on the leading vehicle; however, for those coaches employed on its more significant express workings the Western Region was permitted to use the old GWR colours of chocolate and cream. From the late 1950s No 7020 was predominantly an Old Oak Common resident. This view would have been recorded in the early 1960s, as the locomotive was fitted with a double chimney in February 1961 and would be withdrawn in September 1964. In April 1964 a fine run with this engine on the 3.10pm Worcester–Paddington, loading to 300 tons, saw a minimum of 38mph on Chipping Campden Bank and sustained 70s east of Slough, resulting in a 4min-early arrival at the London terminus. *K. W. Wightman*

Right: East of Sonning Cutting and heading towards Twyford, No 7014 *Caerhays Castle* is seen in charge of an up express on 2 May 1959. Built in July 1948 as one of Hawksworth's '5098' series, it is pictured with an earlier Collett-pattern 4,000gal tender; the double chimney and associated four-row superheater were fitted in February 1959. Initially based at Bristol Bath Road depot, the locomotive would be transferred to the Wolverhampton Division in the early 1960s, following a brief stay at Old Oak Common. Allocated to Tyseley (then LMR 2A) in 1964, it would be among the final three allocated there, continuing to perform well on various passenger duties until withdrawal in February 1965; a typical run during September 1964, between Birmingham and London, saw it complete an untroubled journey from Leamington in 95½ minutes. *Trevor Owen*

Above: The location east of Sonning is again featured as No 5014 *Goodrich Castle* heads towards London with an up express, probably during the early 1960s, as a crew member makes his presence known to the photographer! As will be observed, the coaching stock is predominantly in the original colours of the old GWR company, to which reference is made on page 14. A notable run behind this locomotive, recorded in November 1963 when it was substituted for a failed diesel, was timed at 61½min for the 51 miles between Hereford and Shrewsbury, with a load of 320 tons — an excellent performance for this challenging route. In the autumn of 1957 it had also been one of five 'Castles' chosen to work the 'Cambrian Coast Express', on a 123min schedule to Birmingham. Continuously allocated to Old Oak Common depot in the BR era, it would be transferred to Tyseley towards the end of its career, which would draw to a close in February 1965. *K. W. Wightman*

Right: The 'Pembroke Coast Express', the 10.55am Paddington–Pembroke Dock and 7.45am up working, was introduced in June 1953. In the 1955 summer timetable it made history by initiating the first recorded timing between Paddington and South Wales at over a mile a minute; this at first covered the 133.4 miles to Newport in 128 minutes but was later eased to 131 minutes. Here No 5039 *Rhuddlan Castle* passes under one of the high three-arch bridges in Sonning Cutting with the down train on 19 April 1958. In June 1937 this locomotive, in the hands of Driver F. W. Street, was recorded on the up 'Cheltenham Flyer', loaded to seven coaches, as averaging 90mph for 52.5 miles, achieving a maximum of 95mph at Steventon and passing Southall in just under 49 minutes from Swindon. In December 1946, it was one of five 'Castles' converted to oil-burning, due to shortages caused by the coal crisis at that time, but the equipment was removed in September 1948. *Trevor Owen*

Left: Seen from a different perspective from the usual views at this location, the photograph being taken from one of the bridges mentioned earlier, No 7018 *Drysllwyn Castle* heads an up express through Sonning Cutting on 27 May 1959. Regarded as something of a 'black sheep' due to poor steaming, this locomotive was the subject of ongoing experiments concerning improved draughting and during May 1956 had received a double chimney while retaining its existing three-row superheater. Shortly afterwards it was recorded on an accelerated Bristol–Paddington service comprising seven coaches, equalling some 246 tons tare (260 gross), with Driver Russe of Bristol Bath Road in charge. The 17 miles from Wootton Bassett were covered at an average of just under 89mph, a maximum of 102mph being recorded at Little Somerford; speeds over the Shrivenham–Tilehurst section averaged 88mph, Paddington being reached in 94min — a gain of six minutes over the schedule — the average speed for the whole journey being 75mph. A most impressive performance, it was one of many proving the effectiveness of the conversion. *Trevor Owen*

Above: Seen alongside the Kennet & Avon Canal, near Hungerford on the Berks & Hants main line, No 5055 *Earl of Eldon* heads a mixed formation of coaching stock comprising the 11.30am Torquay–Paddington service on 4 July 1959. It had originally borne the name *Lydford Castle*, but this was transferred to No 5079 in August 1937 and again to No 7006 in 1946. Before the war No 5055 had been one of the locomotives used on the 'Cheltenham Flyer' service and on New Year's Day 1937, despite experiencing strong cross-winds, had achieved a net time of 61.8min between Swindon and Paddington (against a 65min schedule), reaching a maximum of 93½mph, with a load of seven coaches equalling some 218/230 tons. Withdrawal would come at Gloucester (85B) in September 1964. *R. C. Riley*

Left: Another photograph featuring the 11.30am Torquay–Paddington, this time on 26 July 1958, passing the small rural halt at Long Sutton & Pitney, between Langport and Somerton, with No 5026 *Criccieth Castle* in charge. A significant run earlier in the year with a Bournemouth–Birkenhead train loading to 363/385 tons saw this locomotive cover the 19.6 miles between Wolverhampton and Wellington in just over 22 minutes (a schedule gain of 5 minutes), Shifnal Bank being cleared at 47mph. In October 1959 No 5026 would receive a double chimney and associated four-row superheater. Based at Oxford (81F) for much of the 1950s, it would move to Wolverhampton Stafford Road (84A) by 1960, later being transferred to Banbury (84C) before retirement from Oxley (LMR 2B) in November 1964. *R. C. Riley*

Above: No 5029 *Nunney Castle* awaits departure from Platform 5 at Exeter St Davids with an up passenger service on 24 April 1960. From completion in May 1934 until April 1958 this locomotive had been based at Old Oak Common, the highlight coming in September 1957, when it hauled the Royal Train conveying HM The Queen between Newbury and Shrewsbury; reallocated to Plymouth Laira by November 1959, it was to end its working career at Cardiff East Dock in December 1963. As luck would have it, disposal in May 1964 saw it sold to Woodham Bros of Barry, from where it was rescued in May 1976. Subsequently restored to operational condition at Didcot Railway Centre, it has worked various excursions over its old territory, including (in much-altered form) the location illustrated here. *Roy Denison*

In charge of the 9.10am Liverpool–Plymouth working, No 5096 *Bridgwater Castle* departs Exeter St Davids on 19 July 1958. During the 1950s, on a Bath–Paddington express loading to 376/405 tons and despite two dead stands — at the River Avon bridge near Chippenham and at Westbourne Park — this locomotive, under the guiding hand of Driver Johns, covered the 89.3 miles between these points at an average speed of 66.3mph, resulting in a 3½min-early arrival! A Bristol Bath Road engine since nationalisation, No 5096 was transferred in 1961 to Cardiff Canton, moving thence to Cardiff East Dock when Canton closed for rebuilding as a diesel depot. Latterly fitted with an HB-pattern boiler with three-row superheater, the locomotive retained its single chimney until withdrawal in June 1964. *R. C. Riley*

No 7013 *Bristol Castle* passes Dawlish Warren with the 8.55am Wolverhampton–Penzance (otherwise the 'Cornishman') on Saturday 29 July 1961, the Exe estuary being just visible in the background. The siding on the left is occupied by camping coaches for use by the general public; however, these would later be replaced by more modern vehicles, solely for use by GWR Staff Association members, which can still be seen at this location. No 7013 is well-known as the original No 4082 *Windsor Castle*, the change of identity having occurred in February 1952 due to its unavailability to work King George VI's funeral train; when built in April 1924 No 4082 had been driven by his father, King George V, between Swindon Works and Swindon station. Following the changeover the locomotive was based at Old Oak Common, ultimately being retired from Tyseley (by now LMR 2A) in February 1965 after spells at Worcester and Old Oak Common from 1960. The double chimney was fitted in May 1958, while on the smokebox side can be seen the oil reservoir for the Davies & Metcalfe mechanical lubricator, fitted to only five members of the class. *Peter W. Gray*

Heading along the picturesque stretch of line much favoured by railway photographers, No 5089 *Westminster Abbey* is seen passing Parsons Tunnel signalbox, near Teignmouth, with a down express on 9 June 1962. Having entered service in January 1923 as No 4069, the locomotive was one of a batch of 10 'Stars' rebuilt to 'Castle' standard in the years 1937-40. Following nationalisation ex-GWR locomotives — usually 'Halls' — regularly ran passenger services over SR metals, via Winchester, from the Reading direction, and these were allowed to work through to Bournemouth.

'Castles' were prohibited west of Basingstoke, but on Easter Monday 1951 No 5089 arrived at Bournemouth with an Ealing excursion, whereupon it was promptly decided that the locomotive should return light-engine to Basingstoke, where it could rejoin the homeward working, thereby avoiding impounding and further problems! In the early 1950s it was based at Cardiff Canton but around 1959 was moved to the Wolverhampton Division, being retired from Oxley in November 1964. *L. F. Folkard*

Complete with its rake of chocolate-and-cream coaches No 5065 *Newport Castle* heads the up 'Torbay Express' past a number of holidaymakers enjoying some summer recreation, near Teignmouth, on 14 July 1959. This titled train, the 12.0 Paddington–Torquay and similarly timed up working, was first so named in June 1923 and by 1939 was completing the near-200-mile journey in 3½ hours, with just one stop, at Exeter; it was reinstated in postwar form, continuing an earlier extension to Kingswear, in June 1946, completing both journeys in a time just five minutes longer than previously. Although at one time fitted with a three-row superheater, No 5065 would retain its single chimney until withdrawal. Based predominantly at Old Oak Common during the BR era, it was to end its career there in January 1963.
R. C. Riley

Below: Seen shortly after passing Teignmouth (the harbour being just visible in the background), No 7018 *Drysllwyn Castle* skirts the shoreline of the Teign estuary opposite the village of Shaldon with a down 12-coach express on 9 June 1962. Its name had previously been carried by No 5051, being reused on No 7018 upon the latter's completion in May 1949. As noted earlier (page 19) it received a double chimney experimentally in May 1956, being the first of the class to embody this modification. A programme to upgrade the remaining 'Castles' was introduced in December 1957, the double chimney now being combined with a four-row superheater. No 7018 was similarly converted in April 1958 and provided, uniquely, with a lubricator setting that gave 50% more oil than standard, producing an even more marked improvement in performance. It would be withdrawn in September 1963 from Old Oak Common following several years at Bristol Bath Road, during which time it was frequently allocated to the 'Bristolian'. *L. F. Folkard*

Right: The broad expanse of the Teign estuary near Newton Abbot is again featured as 'Castle' No 4037 *The South Wales Borderers* approaches Hackney yard, on the station outskirts, with a down North–West express on 17 July 1959. Built as one of the 'Star' class in December 1910, this locomotive was one of the earlier conversions to 'Castle' standard, being rebuilt (as the consequence of requiring replacement cylinders) in June 1926, some 11 years before the final 'Abbey' series were upgraded. Originally named *Queen Philippa*, it was renamed in March 1937, an official naming ceremony being held the following month. An Old Oak Common engine in the years after World War 2, by the mid-1950s it had been reallocated to Newton Abbot, from which division it would finally be retired. By the time of its withdrawal, in September 1962, it had covered 2.43 million miles — the highest figure for any member of the class. *R. C. Riley*

Inset: Nameplate of No 4037. *T. B. Owen*

Below: Also seen at Hackney is No 7025 *Sudeley Castle*, in charge of the 8.0am Plymouth–Liverpool on 2 August 1960. Built in August 1949, this locomotive was allocated initially to Old Oak Common. In 1960 it was transferred to Shrewsbury and during the currency of the 1962 summer timetable was frequently to be seen on the weekday working of the 'Cambrian Coast Express' between Shrewsbury and Wolverhampton. Reallocated in 1962 to Worcester, from which depot it would ultimately be withdrawn in September 1964, it was among the last 'Castles' to remain in service there, their duties being taken over by 'Hymek' diesels in May 1964 (though steam substitutions continued for a short while thereafter). As such it became one of the locomotives selected to participate in the anniversary run of May 1964, marking the record set by *City of Truro*; as standby at Taunton it was unexpectedly called upon to complete the outward run from there to Plymouth, following the disastrous collapse of train engine No 4079's firebars near Westbury. *Peter W. Gray*

Right: In the less-photographed location at Newton Abbot, alongside the East signalbox, No 5038 *Morlais Castle* heads towards Hackney sidings with the 6.0am Penzance–Liverpool on 19 July 1958. This was another of the five 'Castles' selected at around this time to improve the performance of the 'Cambrian Coast Express' between London and Shrewsbury, including the difficult 1-in-150 Shifnal Bank, south of Telford. Built in June 1935, it retained its single chimney throughout its working life; allocated to Old Oak Common in the early BR era, it moved to Shrewsbury (84G, later 89A) c1958 and would remain based there until transferred to the London Division in 1962, ending its career at Reading (81D) in September 1963. *R. C. Riley*

Left: A busy scene at Newton Abbot on 14 July 1955 as a resplendent No 6025 *King Henry III* together with No 5058 *Earl of Clancarty*, prepare to tackle, within the next two miles, the steep gradients of Dainton Bank with the 10.35am Paddington–Penzance. No 6025 still retains here the single chimney which would be replaced with a double chimney in March 1957; the conversion of No 6008 *King James II* in December 1958 would see the completion of the programme to modify the entire class of 30 locomotives, after the successful experiments carried out with No 6015 *King Richard III* in September 1955. Following their banishment from regular West of England services and, finally, the Birmingham route in 1962 the use of the 'Kings' was much reduced. However, on 17 December 1962, before its withdrawal at the end of the month, No 6025 was noted with a final swansong, heading the up 'Royal Duchy'. *R. C. Riley*

Below: With Newton Abbot's running shed and yard sidings visible in the background No 7022 *Hereford Castle* waits with the 6.10pm return Goodrington–Plymouth working on 5 August 1960. Its double chimney was installed in January 1958. Built in June 1949, it was based initially at Cardiff Canton, transferring to Plymouth Laira in the mid-1950s and then moving to the Worcester Division, via Hereford, in 1964. Another locomotive involved in the May 1964 commemorative trip celebrating the 1904 record run of *City of Truro* down Wellington Bank, it was retained as Swindon standby engine for the homeward leg from Bristol to Paddington behind No 5054, the train having left Plymouth behind No 7029. One of the last four 'Castles' still in service in the spring of 1965, No 7022 was included in a diagram covering an early-morning passenger duty from Gloucester to Cardiff, returning with the 1.40pm Severn Tunnel–Barnwood goods. With Nos 5024 and 7034 it was withdrawn from Gloucester in June, leaving only No 7029 to survive until the end of WR steam in December 1965. *Peter W. Gray*

Above: A further instance of a 'Castle' on 'Torbay Express' duty as No 5032 *Usk Castle* departs Newton Abbot on the down working during July 1959. During the autumn of 1940, on the difficult route between Hereford and Shrewsbury, this locomotive was recorded as covering the 51-mile journey in just under 64min with a 416/450-ton train, while it achieved a measure of fame by taking out the first train of the nationalised era from Paddington, the 12.5am working to Birkenhead, on 1 January 1948. From this time until the late 1950s it was a Wolverhampton Division engine, but from March 1960 it would be based at Old Oak Common, where its career was to end in September 1962. *L. F. Folkard*

Right: Making its way through the Devon countryside at Aller, near Kingskerswell, No 4083 *Abbotsbury Castle* is seen at the head of the down 'Torbay Express' on 8 June 1958. Constructed in May 1925, this locomotive was to retain its single chimney throughout its career. For most of the 1950s it had operated from Wolverhampton Stafford Road depot, but around 1958, probably as a result of the mileage-equalisation scheme, it was reallocated to the Newton Abbot Division. Transferred earlier in the year, it would end its working life at Cardiff Canton in December 1961; discounting rebuilds, it thus became one of the earlier casualties from the main series of 'Castles', wholesale withdrawals not commencing until the latter half of 1962. *L. F. Folkard*

With the starting signal in the 'off' position a well-prepared No 6019 *King Henry V* awaits the 'right away' at Torquay station with duty Z28, a conference special, on 1 April 1962. The bay platforms on the right were normally used for postal and parcels traffic but, possessing an end-loading facility, were found especially convenient for the unloading of animals during the annual visit to the town of Bertram Mills Circus. In the late 1950s, whilst working the 4.15pm Bristol–Paddington train loading to 278/305 tons,

No 6019 attained 82mph through Shrivenham before being slowed by signals at Uffington and Challow; despite this it again achieved speeds of 80-82mph through Didcot to beyond Pangbourne and yet again between Maidenhead and Slough, resulting in a 3min-early arrival at the London terminus. Responsible for this excellent run were Driver Ward and Fireman Merritt of Old Oak Common shed. The locomotive would be withdrawn from Wolverhampton Stafford Road, in September 1962. *L. F. Folkard*

Right: Having completed its journey on the down 'Torbay Express', No 4098 *Kidwelly Castle* stands at the buffer-stops at Kingswear station, awaiting its next duty, in May 1959. Having entered service in July 1926, No 4098 was amongst the first 40 'Castles', completed between August 1923 and July 1927, of which the majority were to retain the single chimney until withdrawal; the first style of piston-valve covers for the inside cylinders, as used on this series, will also be noted. Allocated to Newton Abbot depot for most of the BR era, No 4098 would eventually be transferred to Old Oak Common, where it was to end its career in December 1963. Kingswear station is nowadays the terminus of the privately owned Paignton & Dartmouth Steam Railway. *L. F. Folkard*

In another popular photographic location No 5049 *Earl of Plymouth* (until 1937 *Denbigh Castle*) climbs Dainton Bank on 1 July 1957 with the down 'Royal Duchy'. This title was given in January 1957 to the 11.0am Penzance–Paddington and 1.30pm return working; not a particularly fast train it made several stops in each direction, resulting in total journey times of just over eight hours on the up service and just under that figure in the down direction. Shown here with the tall version of the single chimney, No 5049 had in 1947 been the subject of experiments with a shorter chimney and four-row superheater; although the trials were fairly successful no further conversions were undertaken at the time, and it was not until September 1959 that the locomotive was given a double chimney in combination with this type of superheater. After working in the Newport and Newton Abbot divisions in the early postwar period, it moved in September 1960 to Bristol St Philips Marsh, being withdrawn from there in March 1963. *R. C. Riley*

Heading a rather motley collection of rolling stock, including two ex-LNER coaches, a rather careworn No 5098 *Clifford Castle*, the first of the Hawksworth series, ascends Hemerdon Bank with a Plymouth–Newton Abbot local train on 22 July 1961. This was a further 'Castle' to receive a name previously carried by other class members, in this case Nos 5046 and 5071. It is shown here with a double chimney, fitted, along with associated four-row superheater, in January 1959. During November 1956 No 5098 was among five 'Castles' reported on the SR route via Okehampton (probably the first time this had occurred), having been diverted with the 1.20pm from Penzance as a result of a line blockage at Kingsteignton, near Newton Abbot. For at least 10 years, from 1951 to 1961, it was based at Plymouth Laira; after a spell at Llanelly (87F) it was transferred to the London Division in April 1963, ending its career at Reading in June 1964. *Trevor Owen*

In this interesting study No 6029 *King Edward VIII* is seen at Tavistock Junction on 29 August 1961 with the 12.5pm Plymouth–Paddington service. The final member of this 30-strong class, it was completed in August 1930 and that autumn represented the GWR at the Liverpool & Manchester Railway centenary celebrations; originally named *King Stephen*, it gained its later identity in May 1936, following its new namesake's accession to the throne in January of that year. It received its double chimney in November 1957.

On one memorable run early in 1961, following a late departure with the 2.0pm Leamington–Paddington train loading to 339/370 tons, the locomotive was 'opened out' after passing Banbury; Aynho Junction was cleared at 71½mph, the 1-in-200 four-mile rise to Ardley Tunnel taken at 60mph and a maximum of 92mph recorded at Blackthorn, resulting in the excellent journey time of 85min net for the 87.3 miles to the London terminus. No 6029 would be withdrawn from Old Oak Common in July 1962. *R. C. Riley*

Seen at Plymouth Mutley on its way to Laira depot on 4 July 1957, No 5023 *Brecon Castle* is about to pass No 5048 *Earl of Devon* as the latter marshals two coaches, including a restaurant car, for attachment to the 1.10pm Manchester service from Plymouth (North Road). When completed in April 1934 No 5023 was the first locomotive to benefit from the Zeiss optical system, introduced to allow precise alignment of frames, axlebox guides and cylinders, resulting in a greatly increased mileage between repairs. During the 1930s, with a heavy load of 13 bogies amounting to 401/435 tons and in the capable hands of Driver Street and Fireman Brown of Old Oak Common, it took the 'Cheltenham Flyer' from Uffington to Maidenhead at an average speed of 76.8mph, including a maximum of 79mph near Didcot — an outstanding performance by any standard. Withdrawal would come in February 1963 at Swindon (82C), the locomotive's home since the late 1950s. *R. C. Riley*

Left: With the longest nameplates carried by any ex-GWR locomotive, 'Castle' No 5069 *Isambard Kingdom Brunel* crosses Saltash Viaduct, also dedicated to the famous engineer, as the parallel road viaduct nears completion on 28 August 1961; the train is the 5.30am Paddington–Penzance. On 7 October 1954, in the hands of Driver Hammett and Fireman Luscombe and despite suffering four permanent-way slacks, this locomotive broke a 19-year-old record, reducing by one minute the previous time of 3hr 38min between Plymouth Docks and Paddington with an Ocean Liner Special comprising five coaches loading to 171 tons tare. Constructed in June 1938 and fitted with its double chimney in November 1958, it was based from the mid-1950s at Plymouth Laira, being withdrawn from there in February 1962. *R. C. Riley*

Inset: Nameplate of No 5069. *Trevor Owen*

Below: Also seen on 28 August 1961, having just cleared St Budeaux, No 5058 *Earl of Clancarty* heads an excursion bound for Goodrington Sands, in Torbay. Like other 'Castles' named after members of the peerage, this locomotive had been renamed shortly after construction, its original name of *Newport Castle* being transferred to No 5065. On 22 October 1954 it matched the performance of No 5069 with a similar boat train between Plymouth Docks and Paddington, this time amounting to seven bogies equalling 226 tons tare — much in line with the load of the prewar record trip of 13 June 1935. The 226.8 miles to Paddington were covered in 3hr 37min, and, had the train not been checked twice on the approach to Paddington, a new record could have been established; as it was the 36 miles between Reading and Paddington were covered in 30 minutes. Mainly a Plymouth Laira engine in the BR era, No 5058 was transferred in 1961 to Gloucester, where its career was to end in March 1963. *R. C. Riley*

Left: On an overcast 26 July 1958 No 4095 *Harlech Castle* pilots 'Grange' 4-6-0 No 6860 *Aberporth Grange* as the pair tackle the steep (1-in-68) gradient across Clinnick Viaduct, between Bodmin Road and Doublebois, with an up express. Completed in June 1926, No 4095 was another of the first 40 'Castles' to retain the single chimney until withdrawal; only nine members of this group were to gain a double chimney. At the time of nationalisation it was based at Landore shed, near Swansea, where it remained until the March 1958 mileage-equalisation programme; as part of that exercise it moved to the Newton Abbot Division, operating mainly from Plymouth Laira and staying at this depot until transferred to the London Division in October 1962. Its final allocation would be Reading, where its career was to end that December. *Trevor Owen*

No 7019 *Fowey Castle* stands at St Austell station with an up van train on 8 July 1955. The fireman, in the act of dragging coal forward, has obviously become distracted by the activities of our photographer on the opposite platform! A run behind this locomotive between Bath and Paddington during the mid-1950s with a load of 341/365 tons was described by O. S. Nock as being one of his best on the route: despite two permanent-way slacks an average speed of 72.6mph was maintained between Shrivenham and Southall, a maximum of 79mph being recorded, and Paddington reached on schedule. Built in May 1949, No 7019 would receive its double chimney and four-row superheater in September 1958, some three years after this view. It was based at Bristol Bath Road from new, remaining there until transferred in 1961 to Wolverhampton Division, eventually being withdrawn from Oxley in February 1965. *R. C. Riley*

Left: Starting its descent of Wellington Bank, made famous by the 1904 record run of GWR 4-4-0 *City of Truro*, No 5055 *Earl of Eldon* (featured earlier on page 19), leaves Whiteball Tunnel with the 12.22pm Kingswear–Paddington on 9 June 1962. A further outstanding run behind this locomotive on the down 'Bristolian' was recorded by O. S. Nock in 1939: heading a train of 245 tons gross, it achieved a net time of 61¾min for the 77.3 miles between Paddington and Swindon, reaching speeds of 79-84mph over the Slough–Didcot section and a maximum of 85mph through Box. Built in June 1936, it was mainly an Old Oak Common resident in the early BR era but in the 1958 reallocation programme was transferred to Newton Abbot. Following a spell at Hereford (then 86C) in 1963/4 it would eventually reach Gloucester, from where it would be withdrawn in September 1964.
Peter W. Gray

Below: A grubby No 5073 *Blenheim* passes through St Fagans station, west of Cardiff, with a train of empty vans on the evening of 6 June 1963; the chalked reporting number on the smokebox door relates to an earlier duty. Known as *Cranbrook Castle* until January 1941, the locomotive had its name changed to commemorate the well-known RAF light bomber of World War 2, its original name reappearing on No 7030 upon the latter's completion in June 1950. Early in May 1963 — a month before this photograph was taken — No 5073 was recorded on the 12.5pm Manchester–Plymouth, with nine bogies equalling 325/340 tons. Having taken over the train (from an ex-LMS 'Jubilee' 4-6-0) at Shrewsbury, it cleared the summit of the seven-mile climb to Church Stretton at 37mph and achieved a maximum of 78mph at Craven Arms on the following downhill stretch to Hereford; the later seven-mile ascent to Llanvihangel was breasted at 32mph, before arrival at Pontypool Road, the crew-changeover point, two minutes early. The locomotive would be retired from Cardiff Canton in February 1964. *Alan Jarvis*

Left: Seen posed on Cardiff Canton turntable on 7 July 1962 as a main-line freight passes in the background is No 5061 *Earl of Birkenhead*; another of the series renamed in the latter half of 1937 (in this case in October), it was formerly *Sudeley Castle*. Completed in June 1937, it received its double chimney in September 1958. Throughout the 1950s it had been based mainly at Chester (84K), but following a spell in the London Division it was reallocated to Cardiff in 1960, being withdrawn shortly after this photograph was taken, in September 1962. *John Wiltshire*

Left: In a further scene at Canton depot, standing alongside a sister locomotive on the adjacent shed road, No 6010 *King Charles I* awaits a further duty on a wintry 4 March 1962. It received a double chimney in March 1956, being amongst the first six examples so fitted after prototype No 6015. A Plymouth Laira engine in the years following nationalisation, it moved to Old Oak Common in the late 1950s, being transferred to Cardiff Canton in 1961 and withdrawn in June 1962. *John Wiltshire*

Right: An unusual task for a 'Castle' on a rather hazy 8 June 1963 as No 5056 *Earl of Powis* heads along the main line near Rumney River Bridge, east of Cardiff, with an up coal train. Turned out in June 1936 as *Ogmore Castle* (a name later reused successively on Nos 5080, 7007 and 7035), the locomotive was renamed in September 1937. In March 1961 it was allotted to Royal Train duty, replacing No 7019, when it conveyed HRH The Duke of Edinburgh from Shrewsbury to Windsor & Eton Central. From 1947 based mainly at Old Oak Common, it would be retired from Oxley in November 1964. *Alan Jarvis*

Right: Seen at Marshfield, between Newport and Cardiff, No 4081 *Warwick Castle* heads along the down fast line with an unidentified train on 17 February 1962. The silvered buffers and coupling were especially associated with Landore depot, which used these engines on main express turns such as the 'Red Dragon' and 'South Wales Pullman'. Based mainly at Landore in the post-1948 era until c1959, the locomotive returned to the Neath Division from Bristol Bath Road during June 1961, being withdrawn from Carmarthen (87G) in January 1963. *John Wiltshire*

Paced by a group of enthusiastic spotters, No 5043 *Earl of Mount Edgcumbe* leaves the west end of Newport station with a parcels working bound for Cardiff on 22 September 1962. Completed in March 1936, it had borne the name *Barbury Castle* until September 1937 but received its present title when this name was transferred from the first '32xx' 4-4-0, No 3200. All 13 of the 'Earl' names carried by the '32xx' rebuilds were eventually reallocated to 'Castles' 5043-55, reportedly because some of the personages concerned disliked having their titles associated with such antiquated-looking locomotives! Aside from a spell in South Wales in the 1950s, No 5043 spent most of its career based at Old Oak Common; it moved to Cardiff East Dock in 1962, being retired there in December 1963. Rescued from Barry scrapyard in August 1973, the locomotive is at the time of writing being restored to operational condition at Tyseley Locomotive Works. *John Wiltshire*

Photographed on 8 June 1962, the 8.50am to Newcastle, with two coaches of LNER design leading, leaves Newport behind 'Castle' No 7000 *Viscount Portal*; the absence of a smokebox numberplate will be noted. Completed in May 1946, the locomotive was named after the GWR's final chairman, appointed in 1944. It started life as a Newton Abbot engine and during the 1950s could regularly be found on such trains as the 'Torbay Express' and other passenger services in the West of England. Transferred to Gloucester under the 1958 reallocation scheme, it would end its career at Worcester, moving to this depot for its last few months of service. Unlike the majority of the later '5098' series it would retain its single chimney until withdrawal in December 1963. *John Wiltshire*

Left: No 7024 *Powis Castle* passes its Swindon Works birthplace at the head of a down express on 26 April 1959, a month after an overhaul there which saw it receive its double chimney. During May 1956 this locomotive was involved with the Royal visit to the West Country, together with No 5044 *Earl of Dunraven* taking the Royal Train on the first stage of its journey from Paddington to Taunton. The two locomotives were later used on a further stage of the tour, between Newton Abbot (Aller Junction) and Liskeard, where the train was stabled overnight, subsequently rejoining it at Exeter for the homeward journey to Paddington. Despite the planned conversion of the Paddington–Worcester services to 'Hymek' diesel operation, No 7024, along with four other 'Castles', was still covering several of these in July 1963. Mainly an Old Oak Common engine since completion in July 1949, it would be withdrawn from Oxley in February 1965. *R. C. Riley*

Below: No 5084 *Reading Abbey* at Swindon station with an up passenger train on 28 January 1959; note the oil reservoir (for the Davies & Metcalfe mechanical lubricator) alongside the smokebox. A conversion, in April 1937, from 'Star' No 4064 (originally turned out in December 1922), this locomotive gained its double chimney in October 1958, becoming one of only three rebuilds so fitted. Later that year, despite three severe permanent-way slacks, it reached Temple Meads with the down 'Bristolian' in a little over 107 minutes (against a scheduled time of 105 minutes) from Paddington, having achieved a maximum of 93mph at Dauntsey; the net time was conservatively estimated at 101 minutes. An Old Oak Common resident from the late 1950s, it would ultimately be retired from that depot in July 1962. *Trevor Owen*

Waiting at Swindon for instructions to proceed, No 4092 *Dunraven Castle* is seen in charge of a Class C freight duty on 28 June 1959. Judging by the locomotive's external condition, this was probably a running-in turn following works overhaul. The Hawksworth 4,000gal tender will be noted, as will the 81D shedplate denoting allocation to Reading depot at this time; based at Wolverhampton Stafford Road for most of the 1950s, No 4092 would now remain in the London Division, being transferred to its final shed, Oxford, in 1960. Constructed in August 1923, it would be one of the first 13 'Castles' from the main series to be withdrawn prior to January 1962, this taking effect during December 1961. *John Langford*

Photographed from a down stopping train, a newly ex-works No 6009 *King Charles II* pauses at Wantage Road, heading the two coaches of the 10.10am (SO) Swindon–Didcot local service, on 13 May 1961. This rather unlikely combination could be found on occasions, as Swindon Works often used such trains for running-in purposes, and various large tender engines were regularly so employed following overhaul. During June 1956, due to shortages of motive power at both Wolverhampton and Shrewsbury,

No 6009 had made an unlikely appearance at Ruabon on the 9.0am (SO) Paddington–Pwllheli. (This preceded the special permission granted for a similar working with No 6002 *King William IV*, which headed the annual FRS special to this point on 22 April 1961.) Completed in March 1928, No 6009 would be retired in September 1962, having been allocated solely to Old Oak Common for the latter half of its existence. *R. C. Riley*

Left: During the 1920s a series of trials was held between Swindon and Plymouth to assess the performance of the new 'Castle' class, the result showing the type to be especially economical on coal consumption — a fact confirmed by the well-known comparative trials between Paddington and Plymouth with LNER Gresley Pacific No 4474. On both occasions the 'Castle' concerned was No 4074 *Caldicot Castle*, shown here in green undercoat in the familiar surroundings of Swindon 'A' shop on 1 April 1959. Mainly a Landore engine between 1947 and 1960, it would be withdrawn from Old Oak Common in May 1963. *Trevor Owen*

Left: Having undergone a Heavy Intermediate overhaul, No 6011 *King James I* is seen inside Swindon Works on 14 October 1951. This rare view shows the locomotive painted in the blue livery carried by all members of the 'King' class at various times between 1949 and 1954; this approximated to the former Caledonian Railway colour scheme and was also applied to certain top-link express-passenger locomotives on the remaining BR regions. *Trevor Owen*

Left: Resplendent in the finish applied by Swindon to its overhauled locomotives, No 5080 *Defiant* stands outside the works on 13 March 1955, its 86C shedplate confirming allocation to Cardiff Canton depot. Renamed from *Ogmore Castle* in 1941 to celebrate an RAF fighter of the period, this would be another of the fortunate locomotives to be sent to Barry scrapyard following withdrawal, here in April 1963; rescued in August 1974 and first steamed following restoration in July 1987, it is currently a static exhibit at the Buckinghanshire Railway Centre, at Quainton Road, awaiting a further overhaul before returning to service. *Trevor Owen*

Right: A further view recorded at Swindon, showing No 4082 *Windsor Castle* outside the works on 7 February 1960 following overhaul. As explained earlier (page 23), this locomotive was, in fact, the original No 7013 *Bristol Castle*, the two having exchanged identities in 1952. After the changeover it remained at Old Oak Common and during 1962 was observed covering a diesel diagram, the 5.10pm Paddington–Shrewsbury and 8.42am return parcels duty, probably a result of inadequacies in the steam-heating equipment of the replacement diesels. Withdrawal would come in September 1964. *Trevor Owen*

Below: Making a leisurely descent of Sapperton Bank, between Kemble and Stroud, No 7035 *Ogmore Castle* heads for Cheltenham with a down express, the 2.15pm from Paddington, on 25 June 1962. Its name, as recorded earlier, had previously been carried by three other members of the class, most recently No 7007, which in January 1948 was renamed *Great Western* to mark the demise of the old company upon nationalisation. Completed in August 1950, No 7035 was allocated in turn to the Wolverhampton, Worcester, Bristol and Neath divisions before eventual transfer in November 1962 to the London Division; fitted with a double chimney and four-row superheater in January 1960, it would be withdrawn from Old Oak Common in June 1964. *R. C. Riley*

Right: Descending through the Golden Valley towards Stroud on 25 June 1962 with the 11.45pm Paddington–Gloucester, No 5017 *The Gloucestershire Regiment 28th 61st* passes the small locomotive shed at Brimscombe; this housed the banking engines for the over four-mile climb to Sapperton Tunnel, with its ruling gradient of 1 in 60, and is here host to '51xx' 2-6-2Ts Nos 4108 and 4124, used on this duty. Completed in July 1932 as *St. Donats Castle*, No 5017 had been renamed in April 1954 to recognise the part played by the 'Glorious Gloucesters' in the Korean campaign, the naming being performed at Gloucester Central station by Major General C. E. A. Firth, in the presence of BTC Chairman Sir Brian Robertson and WR Chief Regional Manager Mr K. W. C. Grand. The locomotive would be withdrawn from Gloucester (85B) depot in September 1962. *R. C. Riley*

A rather unlikely pairing as No 7029 *Clun Castle* (now preserved) and '64xx' 0-6-0PT No 6435 (also by now privately owned) head an SLS railtour from Birmingham on 17 October 1965. The pair are seen at Standish Junction, south of Gloucester, crossing over to the Midland route to Bristol from the ex-GWR line to Swindon. Built in May 1950 and fitted with a double chimney in October 1959, No 7029 was first allocated to Newton Abbot, where it remained until transferred to Old Oak Common in August 1962, moving to Gloucester in September 1964. No 7029 was the last of its type to be operated in normal service on the Western Region, being withdrawn from Gloucester in December 1965, some six months later than any other member of the class. Despite passing into private ownership some months previously it continued to work trains on the WR till steam operation ceased. Nowadays based at Tyseley, it is currently (2006) awaiting a further overhaul. *Roy Hobbs*

With a gradient of 1 in 100 for over four miles to the summit, Chipping Campden Bank is the most severe climb on the Worcester–Didcot line. Having just completed the ascent, the unusual pairing of two 'Castles', No 5066 *Sir Felix Pole* leading No 7002 *Devizes Castle*, heads away from the tunnel mouth with the 3.10pm Worcester–Paddington on 23 June 1962; this was probably a convenient way of returning No 5066 to Old Oak Common following an earlier unbalanced working. During the late 1930s, on a seven-

coach Bristol–Paddington train, this locomotive, then named *Wardour Castle*, maintained an average of 78mph over the 65 miles between Shrivenham and Ealing and, despite severe checks at Swindon, arrived only 3½ minutes late. At Paddington in April 1956, to commemorate the late General Manager of the GWR from 1921 to 1929, it was ceremoniously renamed *Sir Felix Pole* by his son, Mr John Pole. It would be withdrawn in September 1962 from Old Oak Common, its home throughout the postwar years. *Derek Penney*

Left: Approaching Evesham, having passed the modernised signalbox which replaced its North and South 'boxes in March 1957, No 7005 *Sir Edward Elgar* has charge of a London-bound working in the spring of 1963. The locomotive had been renamed from *Lamphey Castle* in August 1957, to celebrate the centenary of the Worcestershire composer's birth. Early in 1961, in the hands of Driver Clay and Fireman Edwards of Worcester shed, it put in a first-class performance with a load of nine bogies on the up 'Cathedrals Express', after a delayed start from Evesham the train passed Yarnton in just over 22min (notwithstanding a permanent-way slack at Honeybourne), attaining a maximum of 82mph passing Handborough and reaching Oxford on time. Thereafter speeds were regularly in the mid-70s, and, although progress was slowed by a succession of slacks and signal checks between Reading and Paddington, arrival at the terminus was only half a minute late. *Derek Penney*

Above: No 7002 *Devizes Castle* passes Fladbury, west of Evesham, with an unidentified up express — probably a Worcester–Paddington service — during March 1963. Note that the locomotive now has a Collett 4,000gal tender in place of the Hawksworth flush-sided type attached on construction in June 1946; its double chimney was provided during July 1961. No 7002 was a further example in the '5098' series to receive a name already used on earlier examples of the class, this having been previously applied in turn to Nos 5050 and 5075. Working in the Neath Division, mainly from Landore depot at the start of its career, it was transferred to Worcester around 1960, where it was to remain until withdrawal in March 1964. *Derek Penney*

Left: In this striking photograph, taken against the background of Bradlow Hill, No 7023 *Penrice Castle* clears Ledbury Tunnel with the up 'Cathedrals Express' on 11 August 1962. This titled train, the first such to be identified with this particular route, was introduced in September 1957 and displayed a nameboard that carried a representation of a bishop's mitre. The intention was that, with effect from the Winter 1963 timetable, steam should be eliminated from the Worcester line, and on 7 September 1963 No 7023 would haul the 'last' official steam working, the 11.10am Worcester–Paddington. However, this situation was to be short-lived, due to recurring problems with the new form of traction, both on this line and elsewhere, and steam would ultimately survive until May 1964, pending resolution of these difficulties. Finally displaced from Worcester in June 1964, this locomotive would end its career at Oxley, in February 1965. *R. C. Riley*

Above: No 7026 *Tenby Castle* heads south from Gloucester Eastgate, past Gloucester Park ,on the ex-LMS main line to Bristol, with the down 'Cornishman' on 8 June 1962. The 'Cornishman' title was first applied, unofficially, around 1890 to a broad-gauge express that was then the fastest operating between Cornwall and Paddington via Bristol. Upon the introduction of the 'Cornish Riviera Express' in 1904 the name was dropped, being revived in June 1952 for a service running from Wolverhampton and Birmingham to Penzance, via Stratford-upon-Avon and Cheltenham, on the line through Honeybourne. In the 1960s this represented the longest daily run of any complete train over WR metals, covering 318 miles from end to end, the southbound journey being the 9.0am from Wolverhampton, and northbound the 10.10am from Penzance. Allocated to Wolverhampton Stafford Road for most of its career, No 7026 would eventually be withdrawn from Tyseley in October 1964. *John Wiltshire*

Above: Seen at Worcester on 17 April 1964, No 4079 *Pendennis Castle* prepares to undertake a trial run on a regular Paddington service, prior to its use on the commemorative Paddington–Plymouth excursion of 9 May, on which the aim was to match the over-100mph record set in 1904 by *City of Truro* with the Plymouth Ocean Mail. No 4079 is reported to have attained a maximum of 97mph on the test outing, but on the day would fail to complete the journey, its firebars inextricably melting on the outward run near Westbury. Its place in railway history was already assured, however, this being the locomotive selected to take part in comparative trials with LNER Pacifics Nos 4475 and 2545 in the spring of 1925 between King's Cross and Doncaster; No 4079 put up an extremely creditable performance, especially regarding coal consumption. The locomotive would subsequently be purchased privately for preservation, its more recent history being detailed on page 78. *Roy Denison*

Right: Seen shortly after clearing Reading West, 'Castle' No 7001 *Sir James Milne* approaches Southcote Junction with the RCTS 'Brunel Centenarian' railtour of 2 May 1959. Built in May 1946, this locomotive was the fourth of the '5098' series, introduced postwar by Hawksworth. Named in recognition of the last General Manager of the GWR, it first carried the name *Denbigh Castle*, but this was removed by February 1948 and subsequently allocated to No 7032, completed in June 1950. Here fitted with a single chimney, No 7001 would have this replaced with a double chimney, along with a four-row superheater, in September 1960. Through most of the 1950s it was based at Old Oak Common, but in 1961 it moved to Wolverhampton Stafford Road, being eventually retired from Oxley in September 1963, following closure of Stafford Road depot earlier in the month. *Trevor Owen*

Left: Throwing up a fine spray from its tender scoop, No 7007 *Great Western* passes Goring troughs at the head of the up 'Cathedrals Express' on 4 November 1961; note the highly polished buffers. Constructed in May 1946 as *Ogmore Castle*, the locomotive was renamed in January 1948 to mark the passing of the old company; its original name, already carried previously by Nos 5056 and 5080, was finally applied to No 7035 in August 1950. The double chimney was fitted in June 1961, and by the time of this photograph a Collett 4,000gal tender had replaced the Hawksworth example attached when the locomotive was new. For most of its career No 7007 was a Worcester engine, eventually being retired from that shed in February 1963. *Trevor Owen*

Above: A further view of No 5017 *The Gloucestershire Regiment 28th 61st*, photographed shortly after passing Didcot with an up Cheltenham working on 4 March 1961; the distinctive large nameplate, with its regimental crest, is clearly visible. For a time in the mid-1940s this locomotive was attached to the unique high-sided eight-wheel tender (No 2586) built in 1931, which during its career was coupled to various 'Castles' and 'Halls' until retired with No 5904 *Kelham Hall* in November 1963. Following its renaming (page 56 refers) No 5017 could regularly be found in charge of the 8.20am Gloucester–Paddington service, scheduled to complete the 91 miles non-stop from Kemble to the London terminus in even time. A Worcester Division engine throughout the postwar era, it would retain its single chimney until withdrawal, from Gloucester in September 1962. *Trevor Owen*

Seen near Hinksey South, a resplendent No 7036 *Taunton Castle* heads the Swindon–Grimsby fish empties alongside the infant River Thames on 15 August 1959; newly fitted with a double chimney, the locomotive had recently emerged from overhaul at Swindon Works. An outstanding run with this engine was recorded by O. S. Nock in 1950, when, between Taunton and Westbury, in the hands of Driver Cook and Fireman Hughes of Old Oak Common shed, and with a load of 15 coaches equalling 490/535 tons, the ascent of Somerton Bank was achieved at a minimum of 53mph; the five-mile climb of Bruton Bank (an average gradient of 1 in 122) saw speed fall only from 60 to 40mph, the locomotive showing a remarkable sustained power output, greater than that previously recorded with a 'King' in regular service. In October 1952, piloted by No 7030, it hauled the Royal train conveying HM The Queen and HRH The Duke of Edinburgh to Wales to open the Gaerwen Dam, this entailing a rare visit by WR motive power to Llandrindod Wells. An Old Oak Common resident since completion in August 1950, No 7036 would be retired in September 1963. *R. C. Riley*

Right: Attracting the admiring attention of a local schoolboy, a pristine No 7005 *Lamphey Castle*, with the early style of BR emblem on its tender, waits at Oxford on 21 April 1956 with the 10.55am Hereford–Paddington service. As described earlier (page 61) this locomotive would be renamed *Sir Edward Elgar* in August of the following year, to celebrate the centenary of the renowned composer's birth. *R. C. Riley*

Right: Beneath a fine array of signals No 7007 *Great Western* awaits the 'right away' from Oxford with the 1.45pm Paddington–Worcester/Hereford service on 29 September 1956. On its Hawksworth tender it too features the soon-to-be-replaced early BR crest, sometimes ironically described as the 'cycling lion' or 'ferret and dartboard'. The Hawksworth tenders, lacking a downward-sloping floor, were unpopular with firemen due to the extra work created in drawing the coal forward. *R. C. Riley*

No 6012 *King Edward VI* heads south through Beaconsfield with the 9.20am Chester–Paddington on 4 August 1962. The 'Kings' continued to see service on Birmingham and Wolverhampton trains until complete 'dieselisation' of the route late in 1962, the last four members of the class being withdrawn in December. During 1952, after an indifferent performance on the earlier stages of a journey between Paddington and Taunton, No 6012, with a load of 357/385 tons beyond Westbury, covered the 25-plus miles from Castle Cary to Creech Junction in under 22 minutes, with a 66mph minimum at Somerton Tunnel and a maximum of 76½mph at Curry Rivell. Constructed in April 1928, it received its double chimney in February 1958. In the early-postwar era it was a Plymouth Laira engine but by the mid-1950s had been transferred to Old Oak Common, where it was to end its career in September 1962.
R. C. Riley

Seen in the deep cutting through which passed the separated up line at this location, No 6005 *King George II*, with steam to spare, tackles the two miles at 1 in 167 of Saunderton Bank, in the Chiltern Hills, with the 6.45am Wolverhampton–Paddington on 7 July 1962. In 1948 this locomotive was used in the somewhat inconclusive regional trials held at the behest of the Railway Executive between Paddington and Plymouth and between King's Cross and Leeds; the apparently poor results, relative to fuel consumption, returned by the WR locomotive were a consequence of the less-than-ideal conditions under which it was required to operate. Constructed in July 1927, it was predominantly a Wolverhampton engine in the postwar era, being transferred to Old Oak Common in October 1962 and withdrawn from there the following month; among its final duties would be the final 'King'-operated Newbury Races special workings of 27 October, shared with Nos 6000 and 6011. *Trevor Owen*

Below: Recorded on the same date as No 6005 overleaf, No 5076 *Gladiator* (until January 1941 named *Drysllwyn Castle*) is seen at Aynho Junction with the 10.42am Wolverhampton–Dover/Margate train. This was one of several inter-regional workings that passed through here during the summer period and in this instance is composed of a rake of Southern Region stock. During September 1957 No 5076 was recorded as hauling the 'Bristolian' from Bristol to London in less than 100min, the 77.3 miles from Swindon being covered in just over 60min. Built in August 1938, it was allocated to the London Division from 1960, after several years operating from Bristol Bath Road, and would finally be withdrawn from Southall depot in September 1964. *Trevor Owen*

Right: Making an impressive sight, No 6021 *King Richard II* approaches the summit of Hatton Bank at the head of an unidentified down express in the spring of 1962. During October 1960 this locomotive was unusually recorded arriving at Shrewsbury on a Bristol diagram covering the 1.15pm Plymouth–Liverpool and 7.0pm Liverpool–Bristol return working. Constructed in June 1930, it received a double chimney in March 1957. Aside from a spell at Plymouth Laira in the late 1950s it was based mainly at Old Oak Common, from where it would be retired in September 1962, leaving only six members of the class still in service. *Derek Penney*

Left: In charge of the 4.5pm Wolverhampton–Oxford service, a rather work-stained No 5025 *Chirk Castle* is depicted arriving at Lapworth on 6 September 1959. In 1952 experiments were undertaken with regard to front-end design in an attempt to improve steaming capacity, No 5025 being the first 'Castle' to be modified, along with 'Kings' Nos 6001 and 6017. It was found that, with relatively simple changes, a gain of around 30% was possible, this being confirmed by subsequent tests in service. Withdrawal came at Hereford in November 1963, following a number of years based at Oxford.
Michael Mensing

Left: In charge of an up unfitted freight, No 5088 *Llanthony Abbey*, with some unsightly boiler staining, is seen close to Bentley Heath Crossing, near Knowle & Dorridge, on 30 June 1961. Built in January 1923 as No 4068, it was one of the final 10 'Stars', that were rebuilt to 'Castle' standard, being dealt with in February 1939. It was also one of only three of this series to be fitted with a double chimney, in June 1958, the other two being Nos 5084 and 5092. Postwar it was allocated predominantly to Wolverhampton Stafford Road shed, from where it would be withdrawn in September 1962. *Michael Mensing*

Right: A rather unusual pairing as 'Castle' No 5058 *Earl of Clancarty*, featured previously at St Budeaux, heads Collett '2251' 0-6-0 No 2211 on the 'Devonian', the 12.15pm Kingswear–Wolverhampton, approaching Acocks Green & South Yardley station (between Solihull and Birmingham Snow Hill) on 20 July 1959. No 2211 had probably been attached at Stratford-upon-Avon to assist this lengthy train over the steep 1-in-75 gradient just before Wilmcote and the section of more than nine miles, mainly at 1 in 150, through Henley-in-Arden and Danzey.
Michael Mensing

Right: Heading for the adjacent carriage sidings, No 5091 *Cleeve Abbey* passes Tyseley station with empty carriage stock, probably from a Lapworth–Birmingham Snow Hill local train, on 2 July 1964. A further conversion from the 'Star' class, this locomotive was completed in February 1923 as No 4071, being upgraded in December 1938. One of five 'Castles' converted for oil-burning in October 1946, for the first four months it ran with a suitably modified Churchward 3,500gal tender, this being then replaced by a Collett 4,000gal example; revision to coal firing took effect in November 1948. Allocated to various depots during the BR era, it would be withdrawn from Tyseley in October 1964. *Michael Mensing*

Left: An immaculate No 5072 *Hurricane* heads through Tyseley with what is probably a returning holiday train from the South Coast on Saturday 30 August 1958. Originally *Compton Castle*, the locomotive was renamed in November 1940 to celebrate the legendary RAF fighter aircraft; its original name was reused postwar on No 5099, completed in May 1946. No 5072 was recognised for its hill-climbing ability, and one specific occasion in 1940, recalled by O. S. Nock, saw it sustaining 34mph on the three-mile climb at 1 in 100 through Cattybrook Tunnel from Pilning, the continuation of a similarly steep gradient from the Severn Tunnel towards Patchway. Withdrawal would come in October 1962 from Wolverhampton Stafford Road, to which depot it had been reallocated in the late 1950s, having previously been based at Landore for a few years in the early postwar period. *Michael Mensing*

Below: In charge of the Shrewsbury–Cardiff leg of the 10.5am Glasgow Central–Plymouth service, No 5044 *Earl of Dunraven* is pictured south of Shrewsbury on 24 September 1960 on its way to Hereford; in spotless condition, the locomotive was noted by the photographer as 'the cleanest seen all that day'! Renaming from *Beverston Castle* took place in September 1937, this name subsequently being allocated to No 5068. In March 1936 No 5044 had been the first 'Castle' to receive the more æsthetically pleasing style of chimney; 3in shorter than the type fitted previously (and illustrated on page 36), these were gradually extended to the entire class. In April 1951 this locomotive, together with No 5045, was entrusted with the Royal Train carrying the King and Queen from Paddington to Leamington; as described earlier (page 51) it was again employed on Royal duties in May 1956. Based mainly at Old Oak Common in the BR era, it would be withdrawn from Cardiff East Dock in April 1962. *Michael Mensing*

Upon withdrawal from service in May 1964 No 4079 *Pendennis Castle* was purchased privately and overhauled at Swindon, where it was restored to original livery. Following completion it was employed on various excursions and society railtours, being seen here alongside the erstwhile Midland Railway's main line to Bristol at Churchdown, near Gloucester, with the publisher's outing to Swindon Works on 8 August 1965. Subsequently in the care of various owners, it was sold in May 1977 to a group based on the Hammersley Iron Co's system in Western Australia. However, from October 1994 it languished out of use, and an appeal was launched to fund its return to the UK, this objective being realised with its arrival at Bristol Docks in July 2000. Of undeniable historical significance, this locomotive is now based at the Great Western Society's Didcot Railway Centre, where it is, at the time of writing, undergoing a further overhaul before returning to regular operation. *Roy Hobbs*

After its withdrawal from service in December 1962 the pioneer 'King', No 6000 *King George V*, joined the collection of the National Railway Museum. However, following the intervention of Mr Peter Prior, of cider-maker H. P. Bulmer Ltd, it was transferred to that company's Railway Centre at Hereford for restoration to working order. This resulted in its heading the first steam-operated special over BR lines, between Hereford and Tyseley, in October 1971, following relaxation of the official ban of 1968, when steam haulage ceased on the national railway network. No 6000 continued to operate various excursions over BR lines until 1987, when it was permanently withdrawn for static exhibition, and can now be seen at STEAM Museum of the Great Western Railway. It is depicted here heading an outing for the Severn Valley Railway Association, at Little Stretton, *en route* to Chester, on 23 April 1977. Fortunately the class is still represented on similar excursions by No 6024 *King Edward I*, which will shortly be joined by No 6023 *King Edward II*, also currently under restoration at Didcot, in this case to original condition, with single chimney. *Roy Hobbs*

Index of Locations

Full details of Ian Allan Publishing
titles can be found on www.ianallanpublishing.com
or by writing for a free copy of our latest catalogue to:
Marketing Dept., Ian Allan Publishing,
4 Watling Drive, Hinckley LE10 3EY.

For an unrivalled range of aviation, military, transport and
maritime publications, visit our secure on-line bookshop at
www.ianallansuperstore.com

or visit the Ian Allan Bookshops in
Birmingham
47 Stephenson Street, B2 4DH; Tel: 0121 643 2496;
e-mail: bcc@ianallanpublishing.co.uk
Cardiff
31 Royal Arcade, CF10 1AE; Tel: 02920 390615;
e-mail: cardiff@ianallanpublishing.co.uk
London
45/46 Lower Marsh, Waterloo, SE1 7RG; Tel: 020 7401 2100;
e-mail: waterloo@ianallanpublishing.co.uk
Manchester
5 Piccadilly Station Approach, M1 2GH; Tel: 0161 237 9840;
e-mail: manchester@ianallanpublishing.co.uk

or through mail order by writing to:
Ian Allan Mail Order Dept.,
4 Watling Drive, Hinckley LE10 3EY.
Tel: 01455 254450.
Fax: 01455 233737.
e-mail: midlandbooks@compuserve.com

You are only a visit away from over 1,000
publishers worldwide.